Sojourner Truth

Preacher for Freedom and Equality

BY SUZANNE SLADE

ILLUSTRATED BY
NATASCHA ALEX BLANKS

PICTURE WINDOW BOOKS
Minneapolis, Minnesota

Special thanks to our advisers for their expertise:

Lois Brown, Ph.D.
Associate Professor, Department of English
American Studies Program and African American Studies Program
Mount Holyoke College, South Hadley, Massachusetts

Terry Flaherty, Ph.D., Professor of English
Minnesota State University, Mankato

Editor: Jill Kalz
Designer: Nathan Gassman
Page Production: Michelle Biedscheid
Associate Managing Editor: Christianne Jones
The illustrations in this book were created with watercolor, gouache, and color pencils.
Photo Credit: Library of Congress, page 3

Picture Window Books
5115 Excelsior Boulevard, Suite 232
Minneapolis, MN 55416
877-845-8392
www.picturewindowbooks.com

Printed in the United States of America.

All books published by Picture Window Books
are manufactured with paper containing at least
10 percent post-consumer waste.

Library of Congress Cataloging-in-Publication Data
Slade, Suzanne.
Sojourner Truth : preacher for freedom and equality / by Suzanne Slade ; illustrated by
Natascha Alex Blanks.
p. cm. — (Biographies)
ISBN-13: 978-1-4048-3726-3 (library binding)
ISBN-10: 1-4048-3726-4 (library binding)
1. Truth, Sojourner, d. 1883—Juvenile literature. 2. African American abolitionists—
Biography—Juvenile literature. 3. African American women—Biography—Juvenile
literature. 4. Abolitionists—United States—Biography—Juvenile literature. 5. Social
reformers—United States—Biography—Juvenile literature. I. Blanks, Natascha Alex,
1975- II. Title.
E185.97.T8S58 2008
973.7'114092—dc22
[B]   2007004285

Sojourner Truth was a brave woman who helped many people. She fought to free slaves. She worked hard to win equal rights for women. She used her powerful voice to give speeches that made people think.

Given the name "Isabella" at birth, Sojourner later chose a new name that fit her better. The word *sojourner* means "someone who travels." Sojourner traveled the United States and shared one truth— that everyone should be free and have equal rights.

This is the story of

Sojourner Truth.

A baby named Isabella was born on a New York farm around 1797. Her parents, James and Betsey, were slaves. Isabella had many brothers and sisters. But she knew only her younger brother, Peter. The others were sold by the family's owner, Mr. Hardenbergh. Isabella's parents and Mr. Hardenbergh spoke Dutch. Isabella quickly learned the Dutch language, too.

Mr. Hardenbergh was kinder than some slave owners. He gave Isabella's family a small piece of land on which to grow their own crops. He also gave them a room underground to live in, but it was often cold and wet.

When Isabella was 9 years old, Mr. Hardenbergh died. His family decided to free Isabella's parents because they were too old to work. Isabella was sold at a slave auction for $100. Her brother Peter was sold to a different owner. Isabella's family was torn apart.

Isabella's new owners were Mr. and Mrs. Neely. They ran a small store.

The Neelys spoke English. It was hard for Isabella to understand them because she knew only Dutch. She tried to learn English quickly. Mr. Neely often beat her for not following his orders. After about a year, the Neelys sold Isabella to a fisherman named Mr. Schryver.

9

In 1810, when she was about 13 years old, Isabella was sold again, this time to the Dumont family. She worked hard planting, weeding, and picking crops on the Dumont farm. She also did jobs in the house.

When Isabella was around 18 years old, she married a slave named Tom. Together, Tom and Isabella had five children. Isabella often brought her children into the fields with her while she worked.

As time went on, the antislavery movement in the United States grew. It started changing some people's minds about slavery. New York passed a law that said all slaves in that state would be set free on July 4, 1827.

Mr. Dumont promised to free Tom and Isabella one year early. When that day came, however, he changed his mind. He said Isabella had not finished enough work.

Isabella wanted to be free, so she did extra work for Mr. Dumont. After spinning 100 pounds (45 kilograms) of wool, Isabella decided she had earned her freedom. In the fall of 1826, she took her baby, Sophia, and left the Dumont farm. Tom stayed behind with the other children.

Isabella stopped a few miles down the road at the Van Wageners' home. The Van Wageners welcomed Isabella and Sophia. They gave them a room with a bed. They paid Isabella to work.

At the age of 29, Isabella was finally free. She hoped to find a way to free the rest of her family and all other slaves, too.

In the years that followed, Isabella prayed often and put her trust in God. As her faith grew, she decided to become a preacher. She preached that God loved all people. Standing nearly 6 feet (183 centimeters) tall, Isabella caught the attention of many people. Large crowds came to hear her words of hope. Isabella also became friends with many abolitionists. She joined them in their fight to end slavery.

18

Isabella spent much of her time traveling and sharing her beliefs. She realized that she was not the same person who had been born into slavery. So, on June 1, 1843, Isabella changed her name. She chose the name Sojourner Truth.

Although Sojourner could not read or write, she wanted to make a book about her life. Sojourner's friends wrote down her story as she told it. *The Narrative of Sojourner Truth* was printed in 1850. It became one of the most powerful antislavery narratives, or stories, of the 1800s.

Sojourner traveled to many U.S. states and spoke against slavery. She preached that everyone should have equal rights. Many people tried to stop her from speaking. But Sojourner was not afraid. When the Civil War (1861–1865) and slavery ended, Sojourner fought even harder for the rights of women and freed slaves.

Sojourner Truth died in her home in Battle Creek, Michigan, in 1883. Although she suffered much during her life, she never stopped working to help others. Sojourner will always be remembered as a powerful voice for freedom and equal rights for all people.

1797	Born around this year on the Hardenbergh farm in New York
1806	Sold to the Neelys
1807	Sold to Mr. Schryver
1810	Sold to the Dumonts
1815	Married a slave named Tom
1826	Fled to the Van Wagener home and became a free woman
1843	Changed her name to Sojourner Truth
1850	Had a book printed about her life called *The Narrative of Sojourner Truth*
1883	Died on November 26 in Battle Creek, Michigan

Did You Know?

- No one is sure of the day, month, or even the year that Sojourner was born. Slave owners did not keep careful birth records of their slaves.

- Sojourner gave one of her most famous speeches in 1851 at a women's rights meeting in Ohio. She talked about her difficult years as a slave. She showed the crowd her strong arms from working in the fields. She wanted to prove that women are as strong as men and should have equal rights. This is often called Sojourner's "Ain't I a Woman" speech.

- Sojourner visited U.S. Presidents Abraham Lincoln and Ulysses S. Grant while they were living at the White House. She shared with them her ideas about slavery and equality.

- After Sojourner became free, she lived in Michigan for many years. She helped newly freed slaves find jobs there. People in Michigan celebrate Sojourner's life every year on November 26, the day she died. The day is called "Sojourner Truth Day."

Glossary

abolitionists — people who work to end slavery

antislavery movement — a group of people who worked to end the slavery of Africans and people of African background throughout the world in the 18th and 19th centuries

auction — a sale during which items are sold to the people who offer the most money

Civil War (1861–1865) — the battle between states in the North and South that led to the end of slavery in the United States

preacher — a person who gives religious speeches

slave — a person who is owned by another person

To Learn More

AT THE LIBRARY

Jaffe, Elizabeth Dana. *Sojourner Truth*. Minneapolis: Compass Point Books, 2001.

Leebrick, Kristal. *Sojourner Truth*. Mankato, Minn.: Bridgestone Books, 2002.

Ruffin, Frances E. *Sojourner Truth*. New York: PowerKids Press, 2002.

Spinale, Laura. *Sojourner Truth*. Chanhassen, Minn.: Child's World, 2000.

ON THE WEB

FactHound offers a safe, fun way to find Web sites related to this book. All of the sites on FactHound have been researched by our staff.

1. Visit *www.facthound.com*

2. Type in this special code: 1404837264

3. Click on the FETCH IT button.

Your trusty FactHound will fetch the best sites for you!

Index

Look for all of the books in the Biographies series:

Abraham Lincoln: *Lawyer, President, Emancipator*

Albert Einstein: *Scientist and Genius*

Amelia Earhart: *Female Pioneer in Flight*

Benjamin Franklin: *Writer, Inventor, Statesman*

Cesar Chavez: *Champion and Voice of Farmworkers*

Frederick Douglass: *Writer, Speaker, and Opponent of Slavery*

George Washington: *Farmer, Soldier, President*

George Washington Carver: *Teacher, Scientist, and Inventor*

Harriet Tubman: *Hero of the Underground Railroad*

Martha Washington: *First Lady of the United States*

Martin Luther King Jr.: *Preacher, Freedom Fighter, Peacemaker*

Pocahontas: *Peacemaker and Friend to the Colonists*

Sally Ride: *Astronaut, Scientist, Teacher*

Sojourner Truth: *Preacher for Freedom and Equality*

Susan B. Anthony: *Fighter for Freedom and Equality*

Thomas Edison: *Inventor, Scientist, and Genius*